What Is the SUPREME COURT?

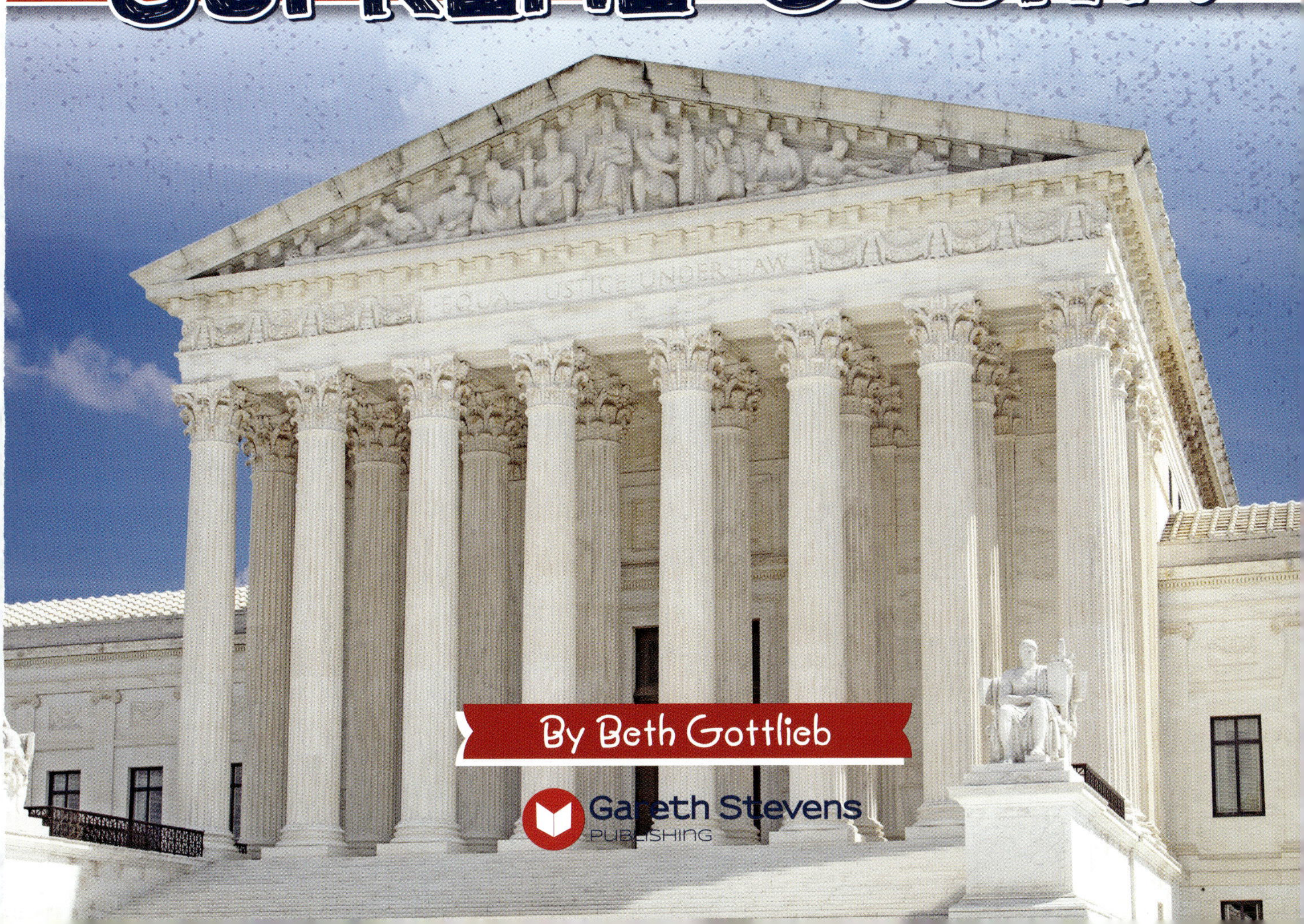

By Beth Gottlieb

Gareth Stevens
PUBLISHING

Please visit our website, www.garethstevens.com. For a free color catalog of all our high-quality books, call toll free 1-800-542-2595 or fax 1-877-542-2596.

Library of Congress Cataloging-in-Publication Data

Names: Gottlieb, Beth, author.
Title: What is the Supreme Court? / Beth Gottlieb.
Description: Buffalo : Gareth Stevens Publishing, 2026. | Series: U.s. government q & a! | Includes index. | Audience: Grades 2-3
Identifiers: LCCN 2024045868 (print) | LCCN 2024045869 (ebook) | ISBN 9781482470147 (library binding) | ISBN 9781482470130 (paperback) | ISBN 9781482470154 (ebook)
Subjects: LCSH: United States. Supreme Court–Juvenile literature. | Judicial process–United States–Juvenile literature.
Classification: LCC KF8742 .G679 2026 (print) | LCC KF8742 (ebook) | DDC 347.73/26–dc23/eng/20241008
LC record available at https://lccn.loc.gov/2024045868
LC ebook record available at https://lccn.loc.gov/2024045869
First Edition

Published in 2026 by
Gareth Stevens Publishing
2544 Clinton Street
Buffalo, NY 14224

Copyright © 2026 Gareth Stevens Publishing

Designer: Andrea Davison-Bartolotta
Editor: Kristen Nelson

Photo credits: Cover, p. 1 Fedor Selivanov/Shutterstock.com; series art (paper, feather) Incomible/Shutterstock.com; series art (blue banner, red banner, stars) pingbat/Shutterstock.com; p. 4 photo.ua/Shutterstock.com; p. 5 (top) Framalicious/Shutterstock.com; p. 5 (bottom) Sherry V Smith/Shutterstock.com; p. 7 (Jay) Gilbert Stuart/National Gallery of Art; p. 7 (Rutledge) File:John Rutledge color painting.jpg/Wikimedia Commons; p. 7 (Cushing) File:WilliamCushing.jpg/Wikimedia Commons; p. 7 (Wilson) File:JusticeJamesWilson.jpg/Wikimedia Commons; p. 7 (Iredell) File:JamesIredell.jpg/Wikimedia Commons; p. 7 (Blair) File:John Blair (page 82 crop).jpg/Wikimedia Commons; p. 7 (frames) janniwet/Shutterstock.com; p. 8 banderlog/Shutterstock.com; p. 9 File:Supreme Court of the United States - Roberts Court 2022.jpg/Wikimedia Commons; pp. 11 (bottom), 21 (bottom) mark reinstein/Shutterstock.com; p. 11 (top) Rob Crandall/Shutterstock.com; p. 13 (inset) U.S. National Archives/Flickr.com; p. 13 (main) courtesy of Library of Congress; p. 15 swatjester/Flickr.com; p. 16 Sketch Master/Shutterstock.com; p. 17 Jennifer Jensen/Shutterstock.com; p. 19 (main) Erik Cox Photography/Shutterstock.com; p. 19 (inset) File:Erich Salomon - The Supreme Court, 1937.jpg/Wikimedia Commons; p. 21 (top) File:Ruth Bader Ginsburg 2016 portrait.jpg/Wikimedia Commons;

Printed in the United States of America

Some of the images in this book illustrate individuals who are models. The depictions do not imply actual situations or events.

CPSIA compliance information: Batch #CSGS26: For further information contact Gareth Stevens, New York, New York at 1-800-542-2595.

Find us on  

Contents

Words in the glossary appear in **bold** type the first time they are used in the text.

Three Parts of Government

The federal government of the United States has three branches. The executive branch is led by the president. The executive branch enforces, or carries out, the nation's laws. The legislative branch is led by Congress, which includes the Senate and House of **Representatives**. Congress makes the nation's laws.

The third branch of the U.S. government is the judicial branch. It is made up of all the federal courts, including the U.S. Supreme Court. The Supreme Court is the highest court in the country.

Supreme Court
Building

The word "federal" means having to do with the
central government. The central government is based
in Washington, **DC**, where these buildings are found.

U.S. Capitol
Building

Government Guides

Founding Father John Adams said of
the three branches of government: "It
is by balancing each of these powers
against the other two that the efforts in
human nature toward **tyranny** can alone
be checked and [limited]."

Back to 1789

The U.S. Constitution is the highest law in the nation. In its third article, or part, the Constitution says the "judicial power" of the country is in "one supreme Court." Supreme means highest possible. The Constitution gives Congress the power to set up this court as well as lower courts.

Soon after the Constitution was **ratified**, Congress passed the Judiciary Act of 1789. This law established the Supreme Court and six justices to serve on it. This law also set up lower federal courts.

The First Supreme Court

John Jay

John Blair Jr.

William Cushing

The first Supreme Court met for the first time on February 2, 1790.

James Iredell

John Rutledge

James Wilson

The Justices

Members of the Supreme Court are called justices. The Constitution does not say how many justices should be on the Supreme Court. In the past, there have been as few as six and as many as ten. Today, there are nine justices.

The Constitution does not list any requirements for who can be a Supreme Court justice. Today, all justices have studied and practiced law. Many have been judges in other courts.

The **Supreme Court** is led by the chief justice. The other eight justices are called associate justices. John **G.** Roberts **Jr.** (front row, center) has been the chief justice since 2005.

Becoming a Justice

The president appoints the Supreme Court justices. This means the president names a person they think would be good for the job. Then, the Senate has to **confirm** the appointee.

First, the Senate Judiciary **Committee** looks into the appointee's background. Then, the committee holds hearings. The appointee has to answer questions about their ideas, rulings they have made, and sometimes even how they would decide certain cases. The committee reports its findings to the whole Senate.

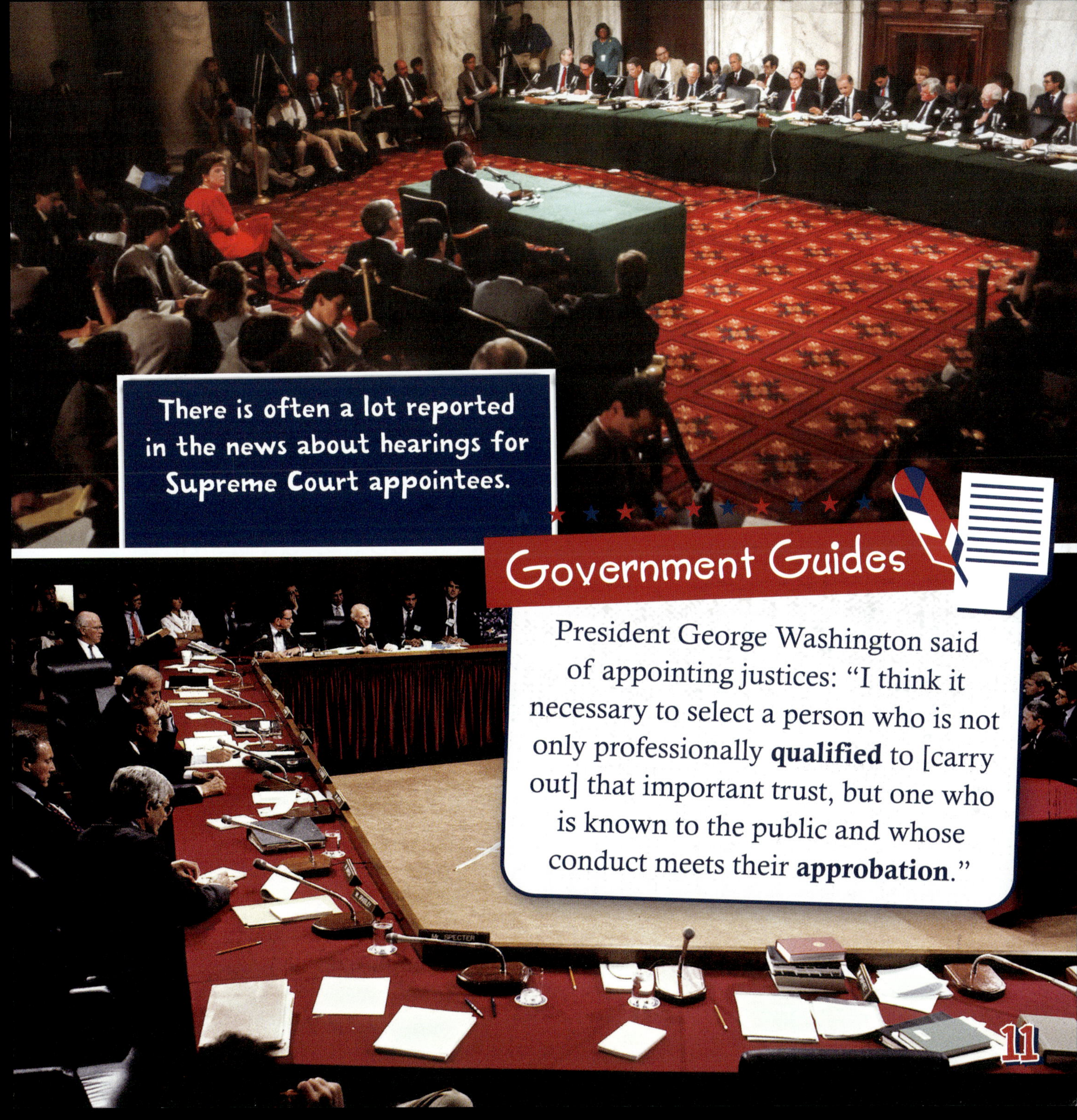

Government Guides

President George Washington said of appointing justices: "I think it necessary to select a person who is not only professionally **qualified** to [carry out] that important trust, but one who is known to the public and whose conduct meets their **approbation**."

Confirmed?

Senators debate, or argue, whether the appointee should be confirmed. After many hours of debate, the Senate votes. If confirmed, the appointee swears **oaths** of office. They promise to be just in their rulings and treat all parties equally. They also promise to do the duties of a justice listed in U.S. laws and the Constitution.

Not all those appointed by the president are confirmed, however. The Senate has not confirmed about one-quarter of those who have been nominated to serve on the Supreme Court.

Sandra Day O'Connor was the first woman to serve on the U.S. Supreme Court. She took her oaths of office in September 1981.

Government Guides

In 2016, President Barack Obama appointed Merrick Garland to the Supreme Court. The Judiciary Committee did not begin the confirmation process at all. Garland did not join the Supreme Court.

13

The Supreme Court's job is to **interpret** laws and the Constitution. It may decide whether a law is unconstitutional, or doesn't follow the Constitution. This is a power of the Court called judicial review. It was established in a Supreme Court case called *Marbury v. Madison* in 1803.

Judicial review gave the Supreme Court a lot of power. A Supreme Court ruling can overturn a federal or state law! Sometimes the Supreme Court overturns its own rulings from the past too.

Government Guides

In 1835, French thinker Alexis de Tocqueville said of the U.S. Supreme Court: "A more **imposing** judicial power was never constituted by any people."

15

Appeals

The Supreme Court mostly hears appeals. An appeal is a case that's already been decided by a lower court, but the losing side of the case has asked that the case be reviewed by a higher court. The Supreme Court is the last stop for an appeal. The court can uphold—or overturn—all or part of a lower court's ruling.

About 7,000 cases are brought to the Supreme Court each year. The Court only hears about 100 to 150.

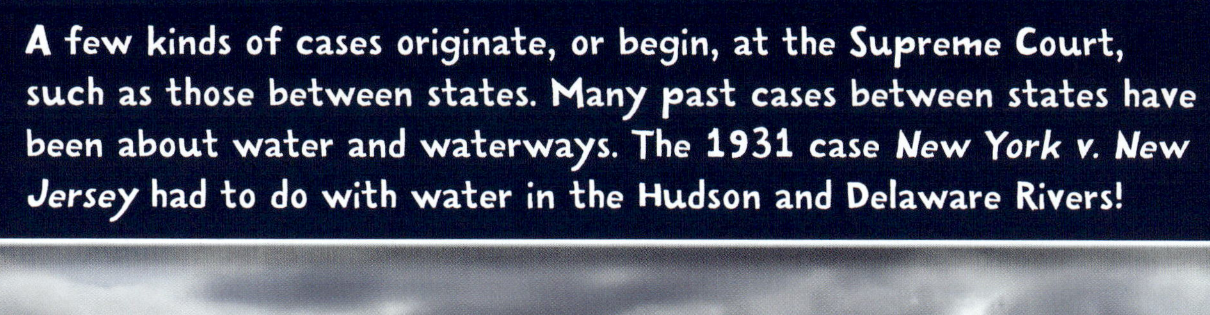
A few kinds of cases originate, or begin, at the Supreme Court, such as those between states. Many past cases between states have been about water and waterways. The 1931 case *New York v. New Jersey* had to do with water in the Hudson and Delaware Rivers!

The Day in Court

The Supreme Court often chooses cases about interpreting the Constitution, important legal ideas, or laws that judges have been interpreting differently. The justices vote on which cases to hear.

The Court learns all about the case by reading **documents** prepared by both sides. They may talk to experts, or those with great knowledge on the subject. Then, both sides of the case often get to present their sides to the Court in person. The justices consider what they have heard and make a decision.

For a case to be decided, a majority of justices must agree. One justice writes the Court's opinion. Other justices may write their own opinions agreeing or disagreeing with this majority opinion. Lower courts look to these opinions to help decide future cases.

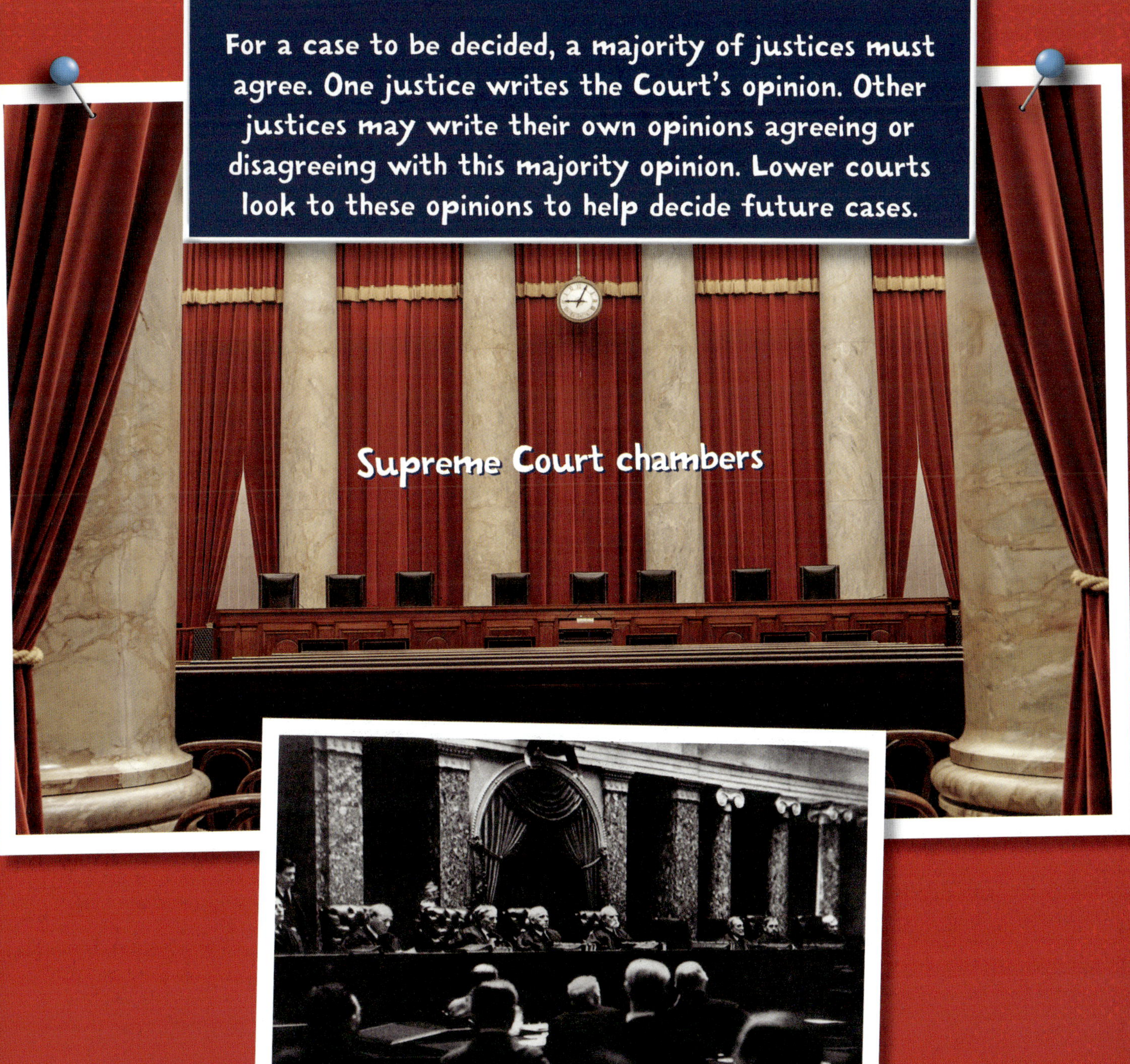

Supreme Court chambers

Supreme Court justices serve until they die or step down. A justice could be removed from office for wrongdoing. However, as of early 2025, this has never happened. The idea behind lifetime appointments is that they can allow members of the Court to make rulings based only on applying the law, not shifting **political** ideas.

There's no question that the Supreme Court is an important part of the federal government. Its decisions affect how the government runs as well as the lives of Americans every day.

Today, some Americans believe there should be term limits for Supreme Court justices. What do you think?

Ruth Bader Ginsburg became a justice in 1993. She served until her death in 2020.

1993

Glossary

approbation: Approval.

committee: A group that works together to make decisions.

confirm: To give official approval.

document: A formal piece of writing.

imposing: Very impressive.

interpret: To explain the meaning of.

oath: A formal promise.

political: Having to do with politics, or activities involving changing government policies or having power in the government.

qualified: Having the needed skills and experience to do a job.

ratify: To give formal approval to something.

representative: A member of a lawmaking body who acts for voters.

tyranny: Cruel and unfair treatment by people with power over others.

For More Information

Books

Finn, Peter. *Choosing Supreme Court Justices.* Buffalo, NY: Cavendish Square Publishing, 2024.

Stratton, Connor. *Supreme Court.* Lake Elmo, MN: Focus Readers, 2023.

Winn, Kevin P. *What Is the Supreme Court?* Ann Arbor, MI: Cherry Lake Publishing, 2023.

Websites

Activities for Students and Families
https://www.supremecourt.gov/visiting/activities.aspx
Find activities and facts about the Supreme Court here.

The Three Branches of the U.S. Government
https://kids.nationalgeographic.com/history/article/three-branches-of-government
Find out more about the part the Supreme Court plays in the U.S. government.

U.S. Supreme Court—Social Studies Shorts
https://ny.pbslearningmedia.org/resource/us-supreme-court-video/social-studies-shorts/
Find out more about the nomination process for justices of the Supreme Court.

Index